BRAZIL
the land

Malika Hollander

A Bobbie Kalman Book

The Lands, Peoples, and Cultures Series

 Crabtree Publishing Company

www.crabtreebooks.com

The Lands, Peoples, and Cultures Series

Created by Bobbie Kalman

Coordinating editor
Ellen Rodger

Production coordinator
Rosie Gowsell

Project development, photo research, design, and editing
First Folio Resource Group, Inc.
  Erinn Banting
  Tom Dart
  Claire Milne
  Jaimie Nathan
  Debbie Smith

Prepress and printing
Worzalla Publishing Company

Consultants
Lêda Leitão Martins, Cornell University; John M. Norvell, Cornell University

Photographs
AFP/Corbis/Magma: p. 25 (left); Mary Altier: p. 10 (left); Nair Benedicto, D. Donne Bryant Stock: p. 8 (top), p. 15 (right); Tom Brakefield/Corbis/Magma: p. 27 (left); Marc Crabtree: cover, title page, p. 4 (bottom), p. 5 (right), p. 7 (right), p. 7 (left), p. 8 (bottom), p. 10 (right), p. 12 (right), p. 12 (left), p. 13 (bottom), p. 15 (left), p. 17 (bottom), p. 18 (bottom), p. 21, p. 22 (bottom), 23 (bottom), p. 27 (right), p. 29 (bottom); Gregory G. Dimijian/Photo Researchers: p. 28 (top); Carl Frank/Photo Researchers: p. 14 (right); Lois Ellen Frank/Corbis/Magma: p. 3; Paulo Fridman/ImageState: p. 14 (left); Collart Herve/Corbis/Magma: p. 25 (right); George Holton/Photo Researchers: p. 16; Randall Hyman: p. 22 (top); Jacques Jangoux/Photo Researchers: p. 11 (left); Wolfgang Kaehler: p. 5 (left); Wolfgang Kaehler/Corbis/Magma: p. 21; D. Komer, D. Donne Bryant Stock: p. 30; Tom & Pat Leeson/Photo Researchers: p. 26 (bottom), p. 29 (top); Larry Luxner: p. 11 (right), p. 17 (top), p. 18 (top), p. 19 (left and bottom right), p. 23 (top); Juca Martins, D. Donne Bryant Stock: p. 31 (left); Buddy Mays/ImageState: p. 28 (bottom); Michael Moody, D. Donne Bryant Stock: p. 19 (top right); Suzanne Murphy-Larronde, D. Donne Bryant Stock: p. 13 (top); Reuters: p. 31 (right); Kjell B. Sandved/Photo Researchers: p. 26 (top); Mauricio Simonetti, D. Donne Bryant Stock: p. 9; Ricardo Teles, D. Donne Bryant Stock: p. 4 (top), p. 20 (right), p. 24; Jonathan Wilkins/Photo Researchers: p. 20 (left)

Map
Jim Chernishenko

Illustrations
Dianne Eastman: icon
David Wysotski, Allure Illustrations: back cover

Cover: The Christ the Redeemer statue in Rio de Janeiro has become an icon of Brazil. The 124 foot (38 meter) tall statue sits on top of Corcorado Mountain and overlooks the city.

Title page: Brazil's coastal cities are known for their long, white sand beaches. Brazilians and tourists crowd the beaches on sunny days.

Icon: Brazilwood trees, which appear at the head of each section, once grew thickly along Brazil's coast. Early explorers brought these trees back to Europe and used them to create a beautiful red dye for clothing.

Back cover: The toco toucan lives in Brazil's rainforests. It uses its large bill to snap up fruit on branches that are hard to reach.

All ready to go! Photographer Marc Crabtree spent several weeks photographing Brazil for this book.

Published by
Crabtree Publishing Company

PMB 16A,
350 Fifth Avenue
Suite 3308
New York
N.Y. 10118

612 Welland Avenue
St. Catharines
Ontario, Canada
L2M 5V6

73 Lime Walk
Headington
Oxford OX3 7AD
United Kingdom

Cataloging-in-Publication Data
Hollander, Malika.
  Brazil. The land / Malika Hollander.
    p. cm. -- (Lands, peoples, and cultures)
  Includes index.
    Summary: Text and photographs portray Brazil's geography and climate, city and rural life, industry, and transportation, focusing especially on the Amazon and the people and animals that live on the river.
    ISBN 0-7787-9338-9 (RLB) -- ISBN 0-7787-9706-6 (PB)
    1. Brazil--Description and travel--Juvenile literature. 2. Amazon River Region--Description and travel--Juvenile literature. [1. Brazil. 2. Amazon River Region.] I. Title: Land. II. Title. III. Series: Lands, peoples, and cultures.
    F2517.H64 2003
    981--dc21
                              2003001265
                                    LC

Contents

The giant of South America

The Tukano people tell a story about how their **ancestors** came to the Brazilian Amazon. After a terrible war, the great Father God told those who were defeated to leave their **homeland**. He promised to lead them to a place where there was fresh, clean water, plentiful fruit, and more types of animals than they could imagine. He asked them to look after the land while he was not there. The people traveled far and wide until they found a vast forest filled with rushing rivers. This was the land the great Father God had promised them. The land was Brazil.

The arrival of the Portuguese

Brazil is nicknamed "the Giant of South America" because it is the largest country on the continent. It covers almost half the land and shares borders with every other South American country except Ecuador and Chile. The Portuguese arrived in this country of tropical **rainforests**, sandy beaches, low mountain ranges, and **fertile** farmland on April 22, 1500. They were led by the sea captain Pedro Álvares Cabral, who claimed the land for Portugal.

Strong winds in the Serra das Andorinhas mountain range, in the northern state of Piauí, have caused the mountains to erode into unusual shapes.

Ipanema Beach, in the southeastern city of Rio de Janeiro, attracts thousands of people on weekends. Visitors swim and surf in the large waves of the Atlantic Ocean.

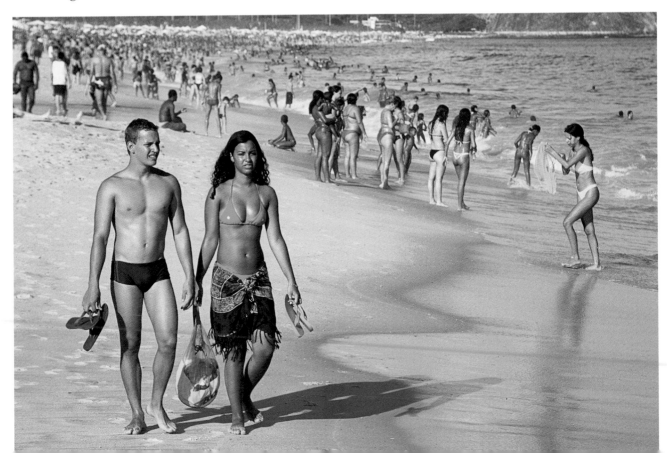

Land of the brazilwood

The next year, the king of Portugal sent explorers to map the new land and search for **natural resources**. The explorers noticed that the country's **indigenous** people used the bark of the *pau brasil*, or brazilwood tree, to make a blazing red dye. The Portuguese king ordered merchants to cut down the trees and ship their trunks to Portugal. The merchants began to call the new land *Terra do Brasil*, or "Land of the Brazilwood," which was later shortened to Brazil.

From colony to country

Brazil remained a Portuguese **colony** until 1822, when it declared itself an independent country. Today, Brazil has 26 states and one federal district, which contains the country's capital, Brasília.

Scarlet macaws mainly eat fruits, seeds, and nuts. They also eat clay from riverbanks, which scientists believe helps them digest unripe fruit.

The market in Belém, in northeastern Brazil, is named Ver-O-Peso, which means "check the weight." This name comes from the scales that vendors use to weigh fruits, vegetables, grains, and fish for customers.

Facts at a glance

Official name: República Federativa do Brasil (Federative Republic of Brazil)
Area: 3,285,618 square miles (8,509,750 square kilometers)
Population: 169,799,170
Capital: Brasília
Official language: Portuguese
Main religion: Roman Catholicism
Currency: *real*
National holiday: September 7 (Independence Day)

When Italian explorer Amerigo Vespucci first saw the Brazilian coast in 1501, he wrote, "if there is a paradise anywhere on earth, it cannot be very far from here." Brazil is well known for its vibrant river systems and spectacular rainforests, but its long Atlantic coast is what first attracted explorers and settlers. Brazil's coastline extends 4,652 miles (7,485 kilometers) along the Atlantic Ocean. Swamps, lagoons, sand dunes, and long white beaches lie along the coast. Islands of all sizes dot the coastal waters, and many Brazilian cities are built on bays and inlets, sheltered from powerful ocean winds and currents.

Coastal climate

Most of Brazil is south of the equator, an imaginary line around the middle of the earth, so the seasons are opposite those in North America. The summer, from December to March, is the rainiest time of the year. Coastal cities frequently experience floods and mudslides. The winter months of June to September are much drier. Throughout the year, temperatures along most of the coast are warm rather than hot because cool breezes blow in from the ocean. Temperatures in the south, however, can drop to a cool 60° Fahrenheit (16° Celsius) in the winter.

The São Francisco is the longest river entirely in Brazil. The Portuguese named the river after Saint Francis because they first saw it on the day dedicated to the **saint**. The river begins 90 miles (150 kilometers) from Belo Horizonte, in the southeast, and flows 2,000 miles (3,200 kilometers) through the dry northeast. The Paraguay and Paraná Rivers begin in the **highlands** in the center of the country and flow south out of Brazil.

Iguaçu Falls

Made up of 275 falls, the Iguaçu Falls sit on the border of Brazil and Argentina, along the Iguaçu River. Water from the falls plunges over a **gorge** 300 feet (90 meters) high. Jutting rocks and small islands covered in emerald green bushes and trees fill the gorge. In the middle of Iguaçu, fourteen falls form the Devil's Throat, creating a mist that rises high in the air. The roar from the force of the falling water is deafening.

The Amazon River and its many tributaries drain into the Amazon basin, an area rich in vegetation and animal life. People live in villages and cities along the river's banks.

Rich in rivers

The Amazon, São Francisco, and Paraguay-Paraná-Plata are Brazil's three main river systems. Each system contains many large and small rivers that are used to transport people and goods. The rivers also provide fresh water for drinking and **irrigating** crops. At 3,990 miles (6,420 kilometers), the Amazon is the second longest river in the world. It begins in Peru, near the Pacific Ocean, and winds its way through Brazil before emptying into the Atlantic Ocean. Along with its **tributaries**, the Amazon drains an area known as the Amazon basin, which covers more than half of Brazil.

The name of Iguaçu Falls comes from a word in Tupi, an indigenous language, that means "great water." The falls thunder down from a height equal to that of a 24-story building.

A community in the sertão gathers outside a home in the northeastern state of Ceará. Few people live in the sertão because the dry climate and droughts make it difficult to raise crops.

The Pantanal

The world's largest flood **plain**, the Pantanal, covers 88,780 square miles (229,940 square kilometers) in three countries — Brazil, Bolivia, and Paraguay. The Pantanal gets its name from the Portuguese word *pântano*, meaning "swamp." During the rainy season, from November to April, the banks of the Pantanal's many rivers and lakes overflow, creating a wetland with small islands of bushy forest. Animals such as iguanas, anteaters, and a type of alligator called a *jacaré* gather on the islands. The months of June to October are the dry season, when the waters recede, leaving an open grassland with small areas of palm trees and other taller vegetation.

The Pantanal is threatened by developers who clear the land for new roads and farms, by miners who pollute the waters with **mercury**, and by farmers who use chemicals that damage the environment. Illegal hunters and commercial fishers are also endangering the wildlife.

The *sertão*

Unlike the Pantanal, the interior of northeastern Brazil is known for its long droughts, or periods when no rain falls. Most of this harsh region is so dry that only a few types of plants, such as cacti and thorny shrubs, survive. During droughts, thousands of *sertanejos*, as the people of the *sertão* are called, leave the area because they are unable to grow the crops they need to earn a living. Cowboys known as *vaqueiros* remain to herd cattle. They wear thick leather hats and pants to protect themselves from the region's prickly plants. When rains finally come to the *sertão*, they are so heavy that riverbanks rise, causing enormous floods that wash away the dry, loose soil.

The toucan's habitat is disappearing as dams are built near the Pantanal and land is cleared for farming.

Brazil's forests

Cedar, mahogany, Brazil nut, fig, and wild rubber trees are just a few of the many species of trees that grow in the Amazon rainforest, in the north and central parts of Brazil. In Brazil's Atlantic forests, on the east coast, brazilwood, ironwood, Bahian jacaranda, and coconut palm trees grow. Seven percent of the world's plants and five percent of the world's animals, including parrots, toucans, giant anteaters, and monkeys live in the Mata Atlântica, as the Atlantic forests are called.

The Mata Atlântica once ran all along the east coast, but it has shrunk to less than ten percent of its former size. The forests have been cut down for timber, farmland, roads, cities, and beach resorts. Since 1986, the environmental organization SOS Mata Atlântica has worked to raise awareness about the importance of the Atlantic forests. **Logging** is now banned there, but companies continue to chop down the precious trees.

The Guiana Highlands

North of the Amazon is an area of mountains, **mesas**, waterfalls, and churning rivers called the Guiana Highlands. Brazil's highest mountain, Pico da Neblina, reaches 9,889 feet (3,014 meters) up into the clouds near the border with Venezuela. Pico da Neblina means "cloudy peak."

The Brazilian Highlands

Filling most of the interior of the country south of the Amazon basin are the steep cliffs, rocky outcrops, rolling hills, and **plateaus** of the Brazilian Highlands. It is here that most of the country's **minerals**, including nickel and gold, are found. Running along the eastern edge of the Brazilian Highlands is the Great Escarpment. The mountains of the Great Escarpment created a barrier that, for hundreds of years, discouraged people from exploring the interior of the country.

The southern grasslands

The grasslands and gently rolling hills of southern Brazil make it an ideal place for cowboys, known as *gaúchos*, to raise cattle and sheep. Crops such as coffee, corn, soybeans, rice, and wheat are also grown in the region. The south is the only part of Brazil with a temperate climate, which means that it has all four seasons. In the summer, temperatures rise to 85° Fahrenheit (30° Celsius), and in the winter they drop below 50° Fahrenheit (10° Celsius). Sometimes, there is even frost or light snow.

The Diamond Highlands, in the northeastern state of Bahia, were once a major mining center for diamonds. Today, people travel to the region to see its caves and waterfalls.

The amazing Amazon

The Amazon is not as long as the Nile, the world's longest river, which is located in northern Africa, but it is considered the world's largest river because it carries the most water. About one-fifth of the earth's water is carried by the Amazon.

The ancient Amazon River basin

Long ago, water at the source of the Amazon River flowed west, into the Pacific Ocean. About fifteen million years ago, two of the huge plates that form the earth's crust collided, creating the Andes Mountains. The source of the Amazon was dammed by a barrier of rock, and a large freshwater lake was created. Over time, the water from the lake pushed its way through the mountains' rock and created a path in the opposite direction, toward the Atlantic Ocean. This is the path along which the Amazon River flows today.

People in the rainforest often travel on the Amazon River in a dugout canoe, created by hollowing out a log. Dugout canoes are light, and travel easily in shallow water.

The Amazon River begins as a stream high in the Andes Mountains of Peru. On its way to the Atlantic Ocean, it is joined by more than 1,000 tributaries, seventeen of which are longer than 1,000 miles (1,600 kilometers). The Amazon and its tributaries are a rainbow of colors. The Trombetas and Jari are the color of green moss. The Xingú and Tocantins are yellow-white from the mud and silt they carry. The Rio Negro is black, stained by the vegetation that grows along its shores.

On rivers in the Amazon basin, cargo and people are usually carried on crowded boats called gaiolas. These gaiolas are moored at the floating market in Manaus, on the Rio Negro.

At some points, the Amazon River is so wide that it looks more like a lake. At other points, the river splits into many channels that wind their way around small islands.

The Amazon meets the Atlantic

The Amazon River empties into the Atlantic Ocean north of the city of Belém. Every second, the mighty Amazon sends more than 52,834 gallons (199,977 liters) of water into the Atlantic, enough for the daily water needs of 2,000 people. The force of the water is so strong that fresh water is found up to 100 miles (160 kilometers) from the coast.

Pororocas

Large waves, from six to ten feet (two to three meters) high, develop at the mouth of the Amazon and travel hundreds of miles back up the river. In Brazil, these waves, or tidal bores, are called *pororocas*. "*Pororocas*" comes from a Tupi word meaning "big roar," which is the sound that the rushing water makes. *Pororocas* are so strong that they rip trees from riverbanks and toss small boats around. Some people in the Amazon ride *pororocas* in canoes, and others surf *pororocas*, a very dangerous sport.

Islands in the Amazon

At the mouth of the Amazon River, water flows into the Atlantic Ocean through many channels containing thousands of sandbanks and islands. During the rainy season, when the Amazon floods, the water washes away sand from the edges of the islands and deposits it farther away, forming new sandbanks and islands. Marajó Island, the world's largest island surrounded by fresh water, was formed this way.

The rainforest

The Amazon rainforest is the world's largest rainforest, covering 2,300,000 square miles (5,957,000 square kilometers). An amazing variety of wildlife lives there. In just 2.3 square miles (6 square kilometers), scientists have found 400 species of birds, 100 species of reptiles, 2,500 species of flowering plants, and 750 species of trees.

Wooden catwalks high above the rainforest floor allow visitors to watch animals living in the tallest treetops.

Layers of forest

From high above, the rainforest looks like a vast sea of green. Move a little closer and a few trees burst out from the "sea." This is the "emergent," or top, layer of the forest, with trees growing between 130 and 160 feet (40 to 49 meters) tall. The next layer down is the rainforest "canopy." Butterflies, vampire bats, monkeys, and anteaters climb and fly among the rubber and Brazil nut trees, which grow from 60 to 130 feet (18 to 40 meters) tall.

At the mid-forest, or "understory," level, smaller trees such as palms, mahoganies, and rosewoods grow. Climbing plants called lianas rope themselves around the trunks of these trees, winding upward to the sunlight. Many animals live in this layer, including sloths and jaguars. At the bottom level, or "forest floor," only herbs and shade plants with large leaves, such as ferns, survive. The large leaves help the plants capture the small amount of sunshine that reaches the forest floor. Dead leaves that fall from the trees line the forest floor, providing food for termites, ants, spiders, and lizards.

Rain, rain everywhere

Many people think that the Amazon is very hot, but the temperature is usually between 77° and 80° Fahrenheit (25° and 27° Celsius). The Amazon is very humid because of all the rain it receives. For about 200 days of the year, rain falls on the basin. During the rainy season, from December to May, it rains almost all day, every day. During the dry season, from June to November, short thundershowers occur. In total, the Amazon basin receives about 87 inches (221 centimeters) of rain each year.

The Amazon rainforest is so large that it creates its own climate. Tree roots drink up rainwater. The water rises up the trees to the leaves, where it evaporates quickly in the heat. So much water evaporates at once that thunderstorms burst out, dropping more water onto the tree roots and starting the water cycle over again. In this way, trillions of gallons of water are recirculated each day.

In parts of the Amazon that flood during the rainy season, people live in houses built on stilts. During the rainy season, they canoe right up to their front doors.

Fishing boats arrive each day in Belém, their nets piled high with the daily catch.

Várzeas

Várzeas are lowland areas near the Amazon River and its tributaries that flood during the rainy season. The birds, mammals, and plants of the *várzeas* have adapted to the flooded environment. Crabs walk on branches underwater; fish jump out of the water to pick food from tree branches; and iguanas dive into the water when threatened, holding their breath for hours.

Cities and towns in the Amazon

About 50 towns, including Acre and Porto Velho, are spread throughout the Amazon basin. The two most important cities in the Amazon are Belém and Manaus. Belém is a port near the mouth of the Amazon River that is built around an old fort. Manaus, which is 1,000 miles (1,600 kilometers) from the Atlantic Ocean, is the trading center for the Amazon basin. Its best-known landmark is the Teatro Amazonas, or Manaus Opera House. The Teatro Amazonas was built from 1881 to 1896, with money from the country's rubber boom. During this time, the Amazon's rubber trees were the only source of rubber in the world.

Operas and ballets were performed at the Teatro Amazonas until the end of the rubber boom, around 1914. It re-opened in 1996.

(opposite, top) Victoria water lilies grow in ponds fed by the Amazon River. The pads are up to eight feet (2.4 meters) around and are strong enough to support the weight of a small child.

13

The Brazilians

Large cities in Brazil are home to people of many backgrounds, including African, Japanese, and Portuguese.

Brazilians are a mix of the peoples who settled in the country over thousands of years — indigenous peoples, people from Europe and Asia, and people from Africa. Many of these people **intermarried**, and their **descendants** follow customs and religious beliefs that are a blend of those of their ancestors.

Indigenous peoples

About 345,000 indigenous people, belonging to 215 groups, live in Brazil. They are the descendants of peoples who arrived from Asia about 11,000 years ago. Some indigenous groups are large, such as the Ticuna with 20,000 people. Other groups are smaller, such as the 202 people that make up the Panará tribe.

When the Portuguese arrived, between two and four million indigenous people lived in Brazil. Many died from diseases brought by the Europeans, such as smallpox, to which they did not have a natural **resistance**. Other indigenous people were forced to work as slaves on sugar

cane **plantations**. Still others married Europeans and gave up their traditional way of life. Today, indigenous people are threatened by developers who take over their land for farming and ranching, and by miners searching for gold and gems. To protect indigenous people, the government has demarcated, or set aside, some of the indigenous people's ancestral land for their use. In other cases, the government has moved indigenous groups off their traditional land onto protected areas. Many developers and miners ignore the laws that protect the indigenous people, and continue to take over their land.

The Karaja people, who live in the western state of Mato Grosso, are well known for their artistic creations, such as this feathered headdress worn by a Karaja chief.

People of Portuguese descent

Most of today's Brazilians are descended from Portuguese who came to the country in the centuries after Pedro Álvares Cabral's arrival. They speak a version of Portuguese that has indigenous and African words mixed in, and follow the Roman Catholic religion, often combining it with indigenous and African beliefs.

People of African descent

From the 1500s through the 1800s, three to four million people from western and central Africa were brought to Brazil to work as slaves. Some slaves escaped and set up communities in the rainforest, called *quilombos*, that were similar to the African villages from which they had been captured. The *quilombos* were often attacked by the military, and their inhabitants were killed or returned to slavery. When the slaves were freed in 1888, many became farmers or started businesses such as restaurants and barbershops. Others made and sold crafts. Most of the former slaves stayed in the northeast, particularly in the state of Bahia. Their descendants still live there, influencing the region's food, music, dance, and celebrations.

Japanese women wear traditional kimonos at a celebration marking the date on which the first Japanese arrived in Brazil, June 18, 1908.

Recent immigrants

After slavery was abolished in 1888, Brazil's government encouraged people from Portugal and other European countries to immigrate to Brazil. Many Germans and Italians moved to the south, where they worked on coffee plantations and established small farms.

Beginning in 1908, Europeans in Brazil were joined by Japanese who moved because there was not enough food for Japan's growing population. Today, there are more Japanese in Brazil than in any other country except Japan. About one million Brazilians have Japanese ancestry. The majority of them live in the southeastern city of São Paulo. In the past 25 years, about 700,000 people from Syria, Lebanon, and other parts of the Middle East have also come to Brazil. Like the Japanese, most settled in São Paulo.

This woman from Salvador wears the colorful full skirt and headdress of Baianas, or women from Bahia.

Coastal cities

Although Brazil has an abundance of land in the interior, most of its large cities are on the Atlantic coast. Many are ports from which products such as coffee, orange juice, and steel are shipped around the world. One exception is the capital city of Brasília, located about 560 miles (900 kilometers) from the Atlantic.

Brasília

Brasília was planned by the government to encourage people to move inland, so they could develop the region's rich natural resources. Construction of the city began in 1956, and the city was inaugurated, or opened for use by the public, on April 21, 1960.

Brasília was designed by city planner Lúcio Costa. It is shaped like an airplane. The body of the plane is made up of government buildings, and the wings are made up of large squares called *superquadras*. Each *superquadra* has tall apartment buildings, schools, shops,

restaurants, and large fields for relaxing and playing sports. Unlike other cities, Brasília has long, sweeping highways with no intersections or street corners. To get from one area to another, people must drive, take a bus, or walk in underground tunnels.

Busy São Paulo

Brazil's largest city, São Paulo, sits more than 2,000 feet (610 meters) above sea level. It is the capital of the state of São Paulo. It was established in 1554 as a mission, where Catholic priests preached and **converted** indigenous people. In the 1600s, adventurers called *bandeirantes* used São Paulo as a base from which they traveled into Brazil's interior to search for slaves, gold, and gems. In the past century, the city has grown because of the coffee trade and because of the many industries established there. Including the suburbs, São Paulo now has a population of almost 18 million, making it one of the world's largest cities.

(top) Brasília's buildings were designed to look completely different from buildings in other Brazilian cities. The National Congress is made up of two tall towers, which hold offices, and two "domes" with circular seating. Politicians in the National Congress meet to discuss Brazil's laws.

Most people in downtown São Paulo live in high-rise apartment buildings because there is so little room for houses.

Cities within a city

São Paulo is home to many **ethnic** neighborhoods. Bela Vista is the Italian neighborhood. In August, it hosts a huge festival, the *Festa da Nossa Senhora Acheropita*, with Italian music, dancing, and tons of pizza and spaghetti! In Vinte e Cinco de Março, Arab restaurants and stores sell food and clothing from Lebanon, Syria, and Turkey.

Beautiful Rio de Janeiro

The Italian explorer Amerigo Vespucci was the first European to land at Guanabara Bay, on Brazil's southeastern coast. He named the area Rio de Janeiro, which means "River of January," because he thought the bay was a river and because he arrived on January 1. By 1567, the Portuguese had established a town by the bay called São Sebastião do Rio de Janeiro, which soon became known as Rio de Janeiro. Rio became Brazil's capital in 1763, when the region prospered from the discovery of gold and diamonds. It remained the capital until 1960, when Brasília was inaugurated. It is still the capital of the state of Rio de Janeiro.

Carved out of mountains

Rio de Janeiro was carved out of the rainforest-covered mountains surrounding the bay. The most famous mountain is Sugar Loaf, at the entrance to Guanabara Bay. This cone-shaped, granite peak looks like the clay molds the Portuguese once used to purify sugar.

Sugar Loaf Mountain stands at the entrance to Guanabara Bay. The bay's white, sandy beaches, including Copacabana and Ipanema, are popular places for cariocas, as the people of Rio are called, to swim, play, read, relax, and eat.

Salvador, the city of gold

Founded in 1549, Salvador, on the northeastern coast, was Brazil's first capital. It was the center of Brazil's African slave trade, and the main port from which sugar, gold, and gems were **exported**. Many of Salvador's beautiful mansions and churches are decorated with gold, including the Igreja São Francisco, or Church of Saint Francis.

Salvador, which is the capital of the state of Bahia, is built on two levels. At sea level is the Cidade Baixa, or Lower City, with the port and main markets. The Cidade Alta, or Upper City, sits on a cliff 234 feet (71 meters) above sea level. It is the historic part of Salvador, with churches, mansions, and museums. To get to the Cidade Alta from the Cidade Baixa, people walk, take an elevator, or take a funicular, a railway car attached to a cable which goes up and down the cliff.

(above) At the peak of Corcovado Mountain, in the northern part of Rio de Janeiro, a statue of Christ the Redeemer holds out its arms as if to embrace the city. Completed in 1932, the granite statue is 124 feet (38 meters) tall and weighs 700 tons (635 metric tons).

(below) Colorful colonial-style buildings line the sloping streets of Salvador's Pelarino area. The city was built on two levels, the Lower City and the Upper City, and sits on a cliff above the sea.

Tall hotels line the beach area known as Boa Viagem, in Recife. Many people visit Recife to snorkel in its coral reefs, where colorful fish, coral, and underwater plants live.

Recife

Recife, on the northeastern coast, is Brazil's fourth largest city and the capital of the state of Pernambuco. Old churches and markets from colonial times mix with the modern buildings of the financial district. One of the city's most interesting buildings, Casa da Cultura de Pernambuco, used to be the city's prison. Now, it is an arts and crafts center, where each former prisoner's cell is a small shop. Recife is also known for the canals, or channels of water, and bridges that link its three main islands. It is also known for the **reefs** found close to shore. In fact, Recife got its name from the Portuguese word *arrecife*, which means "barrier reef."

Belo Horizonte, in southeastern Brazil, is the country's third largest city. It stands on a high plateau, 2,500 feet (762 meters) above sea level.

Porto Alegre

Porto Alegre is the largest city in southern Brazil and the capital of the state of Rio Grande do Sul. Portuguese colonists founded Porto Alegre, first known as Porto dos Casais, in 1742. German immigrants settled in the area in 1825, and were soon joined by immigrants from Italy and Poland. Porto Alegre has many factories that process products from farms nearby, including meat, hides, wool, and beans. It is also a center for shipbuilding and for manufacturing electrical equipment.

The citizens of Porto Alegre help decide what improvements to make in their communities, such as building or restoring plazas where people relax during their free time.

From farms, forests, and oceans

The brazilwood tree, which the indigenous people and the Portuguese used to make red dye, was Brazil's first important export in the 1500s. By the end of that century, about a hundred ships sailed every year to Portugal loaded with brazilwood. Portuguese colonists also established plantations along the coast where they grew first sugar cane, then cotton, and then coffee beans. Today, Brazil provides one-fourth of the world's coffee, and exports large quantities of sugar.

Fresh fruit and more

In many areas of the south and southeast, a moderate amount of rain falls and it does not get very hot or very cold. Crops such as wheat, corn, and rice grow well in these areas, as do soybeans, used mostly to feed cattle, and coffee beans. A variety of fruit trees and vines also thrive there, providing papayas; passionfruit; yellow or green pear-shaped fruit called *goiabas*; *graviolas*, which are large oval fruit that taste like a combination of pineapples and bananas; and grapes for eating and making wine. In the northeast, cocoa beans, used to make chocolate, and sugar cane, made into raw sugar, grow well in the hotter, drier climate.

Workers at this agricultural warehouse in São Paulo sort fruit and vegetables before they are sent to stores for sale.

Gifts from the rainforest

Brazil's rainforests are full of trees and plants that have many uses. The strong, colorful woods from reddish-brown mahoganies, fragrant jacarandas, rosewoods, and Amazonian cedars are used to make furniture, musical instruments, and household items such as salad bowls. Perfumes, flavorings, and medicine are made from trees and plants. Curare, from a woody, climbing vine, is used to stop pain and to relax muscles before surgery. Quinine, from the cinchona tree, is prescribed for a disease called malaria.

A coffee harvester pours a load of coffee beans into a basket, which is used to measure a day's picking. Later, workers separate ripe coffee beans, which are shiny and red, from unripe beans, which are green.

Harvesting Brazil nuts

The Brazil nut, or *castanha-do-pará*, is the edible seed of the Brazil nut tree. The nuts grow in pods that look like large coconuts. Each pod weighs up to 5 pounds (2.3 kilograms) and holds 12 to 24 nuts. During Brazil nut season, from January to June, the pods ripen and fall to the ground, where people called *castanheiros* harvest them. Waiting for the pods to fall is much easier than climbing the 150-foot (45-meter) trees to collect them.

Castanheiros split open the pods with large, heavy knives called machetes and lay the brazil nuts in the sun to dry. The large nuts are eaten whole or chopped up and used in different foods and drinks. The oil from the nuts is used in shampoos, soaps, and other skincare products.

A rubber tapper uses a sharp knife to cut notches in the bark of a rubber tree. White latex oozes out of the notches into a cup attached to the tree. The latex is heated and processed to make rubber.

The rubber boom

For hundreds of years, indigenous people have used a white liquid sap from rubber trees, called latex, as a waterproofing material for canoes. They heated the latex over a fire, thickening it into raw rubber. By the mid 1800s, people around the world wanted rubber to make balls, bottles, and footwear. Huge areas of the rainforest were cleared to grow more rubber trees.

Brazil was the world's only source of rubber until 1876, when a British traveler smuggled rubber tree seedlings out of Brazil. The seedlings were carefully replanted on plantations in Ceylon, which is present-day Sri Lanka. By 1910, these plantations were producing more rubber at cheaper prices than Brazil. Most countries stopped buying Brazilian rubber, and Brazil's rubber boom ended.

A vaqueiro, *or cowboy, watches over herds of cattle in the Pantanal.*

Cattle are king

Pigs, sheep, goats, and chickens are all raised in Brazil, but cattle is the country's most important **livestock**. With 153 million cattle on thousands of ranches, Brazil has one-quarter of the world's cattle. Most of the beef and dairy cattle are raised in the south, where they graze on the region's vast grasslands. The pasturelands in the northeast, called *campos*, are of poorer quality. Many cattle in that region are raised for their hides, which are used to make leather. In the Amazon basin, large areas of rainforest have been cleared for cattle ranches. Some of the beef produced in the Amazon feeds the people of Brazil, but much of it is sold to international hamburger companies.

Fresh fish from the sea

In the northeast, Brazilian fishers sail in small boats, called *jangadas*, to catch tuna, cod, lobster, and shrimp. *Jangadas* are made of logs or plastic tubes roped together, and have large, colorful sails. Until recently, most of the fish caught were eaten locally. Today, commercial trawlers travel far out in the ocean and use wide nets to catch tuna and lobster for export. Commercial fishing also takes place in the country's many rivers, including the rivers of the Pantanal, where the stocks of fish are decreasing. The government has set limits on how many fish can be caught there.

Fishers gather their nets on a beach in Natal, in the northeast. Some fishers use the latest electronic equipment to locate fish, while others use more traditional methods of fishing.

Mining and manufacturing

Since the 1970s, Brazil's manufacturing and service industries, such as construction, retail, and tourism, have become a large part of the country's economy. Many people from rural Brazil left their farms and moved to cities to find work. Brazil borrowed a great deal of money from banks overseas to help its industries grow. By the early 1990s, it was unable to pay back the money it owed. Prices of food, clothing, and gasoline rose every day, and Brazilian money became worthless compared to other **currencies**.

The *Plano Real*

In 1994, Brazil's government introduced the *Plano Real*, or *Real* Plan, to help the economy. Under the plan, government spending decreased; a new currency, the *real*, was introduced; prices dropped; Brazilian businesses started to modernize; foreign companies opened factories in Brazil; new jobs were created; and salaries rose. The Treaty of Asuncíon, which was signed in 1991 by Brazil, Argentina, Paraguay, and Uruguay, also helped Brazil's economy. The treaty made it easier for those countries to trade with one another. Even with these improvements, Brazil's economy is still in trouble. Brazil owes large amounts of money to other countries, and one-third of its population cannot afford enough food, a place to live, or land to farm.

Manufacturing

Most of Brazil's industrial areas are in the southeast, around the cities of São Paulo, Rio de Janeiro, and Belo Horizonte. Factories in this region produce more than one million cars and trucks a year, as well as airplanes, ships, televisions, radios, refrigerators, air conditioners, and computers. Some industries process farm products: sugar cane becomes sugar, cotton is made into fabric, and oranges are squeezed into orange juice. New industries have created jobs for Brazilians, but they have also created a major problem — air and water pollution.

Steel is heated and rolled into strips at an industrial plant in São Bernardo do Campo, in the southeast. The steel is then used to make cars, ships, computers, and other products at factories in Brazil.

Brazil is a popular destination for tourists. These tourists are hoping to spot macaws, toucans, and other rainforest birds along the shores of the Amazon River.

23

Travel to Brazil

Two million people from around the world travel to Brazil each year to experience its culture and natural beauty. Festivals full of music, dance, food, and parades draw visitors to Rio de Janeiro, Salvador, and many other cities and towns. In the Amazon and the Pantanal, the ecotourism industry provides visitors with the opportunity to see rare and endangered animals, trees, and plants in their natural environment. Mineral springs, where people bathe in warm water that bubbles up from underground, are popular tourist destinations. Many people believe that the minerals in the springs relieve sore muscles and cure high blood pressure and poor digestion.

Gold rush

For almost 200 years after the Portuguese arrived in Brazil, very few non-indigenous people traveled into the interior. This changed when gold was discovered in the southeastern state of Minas Gerais in 1695 and in the western state of Mato Grosso in 1719. Many Brazilians left their homes for the interior states, hoping to quickly make their fortunes from gold. Towns were built almost overnight to accommodate the **prospectors**. By 1760, almost half the world's gold came from Brazil's mines, but by 1770, most of the gold had been **extracted** and the gold rush ended. A second gold rush began in 1979, when gold was discovered in the state of Pará. Since then, prospectors, called *garimpeiros*, have also found gold in the Amazon states of Roraima and Rondônia.

Minerals, metals, and gems

Gold is not the only valuable product mined in Brazil. The country has large deposits of iron ore, which is used to make steel; cassiterite, which is used to make tin; and bauxite, which is used to make aluminum. People all over the world wear jewelry with gems from Brazil: sparkling diamonds, bright green emeralds, yellow topazes, purple amethysts, and bluish-green aquamarines. One of the world's largest quartz crystal deposits lies in Cristalina, near Brasília. Quartz crystal is used in watches and clocks.

Miners extract limestone, a rock used to construct buildings and monuments, in the northeastern state of Piauí.

A mine worker at Grande Carajás examines the area's red soil, which is rich in iron.

Grande Carajás

In 1967, a Brazilian **geologist** working for an American steel company was forced to land his helicopter on top of a hill in the Serra dos Carajás, a mountain range in Pará. Imagine his surprise when he realized that he had landed on solid iron ore. In fact, he had discovered the largest iron ore deposit in the world. The Serra dos Carajás also contains copper, gold, and other valuable minerals.

The government developed a mining project called Grande Carajás, which covers an area more than twice the size of California. It includes iron and aluminum smelting plants, where ore from the mines is melted to extract minerals. Although Grande Carajás has provided many people with jobs, a large area of rainforest, with plants and animals found nowhere else on earth, was destroyed. As well, many indigenous people were forced to move.

The Tucuruí hydroelectric plant is one of the largest hydroelectric projects in the world. Large amounts of rainforest were flooded to build the plant, destroying thousands of farms and dozens of towns.

Water power

Dams built along some of Brazil's rivers use the fast-flowing water as a source of energy called hydroelectricity. More than 90 percent of Brazil's electricity is produced by two hydroelectric projects: the Tucuruí hydroelectric dam, on the Tocantins River in the Amazon basin, and the Itaipu hydroelectric dam, on the Paraná River in the south. Brazil and Paraguay built the Itaipu dam together between 1975 and 1984. Itaipu is 4,900 feet (1,495 meters) high. Its eighteen **turbines** generate more electricity than any other hydroelectric plant in the world. The plant is so big that during construction the Brazil National Orchestra gave a concert inside one of Itaipu's **generators**!

A small amount of Brazil's energy comes from coal, gas, oil, and **nuclear power** plants. Many Brazilians power their cars with *alcool*. *Alcool* is produced by combining ethanol, made from sugar cane, with small amounts of gasoline. It is cheaper than gasoline and creates less pollution.

Animals of the Amazon

Scientists believe that the many different plants and animals in the Amazon developed as a result of small changes in the climate over the past ten million years. Areas near the equator, including Brazil, experienced a small drop in temperature and less rainfall. Parts of the Amazon became grasslands that surrounded large "islands" of trees and plants. Over time, the animals on each "island" developed different colored fur, feathers, or skin, and became different sizes than the same animals on other "islands." So far, scientists have found more than 1,600 types of birds, 3,000 kinds of fish, 230 kinds of snakes, 600 kinds of mammals, 70,000 types of insects, and 40 kinds of turtles in the Amazon. They estimate that millions more species of plants and animals have yet to be discovered.

Morpho butterflies are larger than a person's hand, with a wingspan of up to 7 inches (18 centimeters).

The golden lion tamarin, a type of monkey found only in Brazil, has a strong, flexible tail that helps it balance as it moves from branch to branch.

Howlers and more

High up in the rainforest's treetops, the large howler monkey cries out so loudly that it can be heard more than two miles (3.2 kilometers) away. The sloth spends almost all its time sleeping while hanging upside down from tree branches. About once a week, it comes down to the forest floor to eliminate waste from its system. The anteater walks on its knuckles along the forest floor, crushing ant and termite nests with its strong paws. Then, it uses its long, sticky tongue to catch and eat the insects. The jaguar uses its large muzzle and ability to swim to help it catch and devour deer, tapirs, capybaras, and caimans, a kind of alligator.

Capybaras

Capybaras are the world's largest rodents. They weigh between 77 and 145 pounds (35 and 66 kilograms) and grow to between three and four feet (0.9 and 1.2 meters) long. Their hog-like bodies are covered in thin brownish-red hair, and their faces look like guinea pigs' faces. Capybaras communicate with each other by whistling and making barking sounds. They feed on water plants and grasses, and protect the area where they live by releasing a strong scent from their scent glands.

Capybaras' front legs are shorter than their back legs, making them clumsy walkers, but their webbed feet make them good swimmers.

An anaconda swallows its prey head first and digests it very slowly. After a large meal, an anaconda can go for up to two years without eating.

Harmless and poisonous snakes

Hiding in the Amazon's thick vegetation is the poisonous bushmaster snake. When the bushmaster bites, it injects up to 1.4 ounces (40 milliliters) of poison that destroys its prey's **nervous system**. Another poisonous snake, the fer-de-lance, has a heat sensor below its eyes so it can tell if its prey is close by. The anaconda is the world's largest snake. It can grows up to 29 feet (8.8 meters), weighs up to 550 pounds (250 kilograms), and becomes as thick as a telephone pole. The anaconda is one of the many snakes that rarely harms people, but it often makes a meal out of jaguars, capybaras, caimans, and other large animals.

Bats that feed on fruit and blood

Bats in the Amazon hang in caves or in the holes of trees. Many species eat only insects and fruit, but the fringe-lipped bat eats frogs. It can identify different frogs' mating calls and recognize frogs that are poisonous or too large to eat. Vampire bats use their very sharp teeth to make cuts on the skin of large mammals, then they lap up the blood that flows out. One vampire bat can eat up to two ounces (57 milliliters) of blood in one night.

Leaf cutter ants carry pieces of leaves across the forest floor and back to their nest. Each trip takes the ants several hours.

Indigenous people rub the tips of their arrows, which they use to hunt, over the skin of poison arrow frogs. Then, the hunters use the poisoned arrows to catch birds, monkeys, and other animals.

Fantastic frogs

Frogs are some of the most colorful animals in the Amazon. Poison arrow frogs are sometimes called "painted frogs" because of their bright red, blue, or green skin, which warns **predators** that they are poisonous. Glass frogs have transparent skin on their bellies so you can see their insides. Pygmy marsupial frogs have large webbed feet and toes that cling to the leaves and branches where they live. They carry their eggs in a pouch attached to their backs. When the eggs become tadpoles, the frogs release them into the water.

Amazon insects

Marching across the rainforest floor are armies of leaf cutter ants carrying leaves they cut up with their saw-toothed jaws. These ants, which can carry 50 times their weight, chew the leaves to make a paste in which **fungus** grows. The ants then eat the fungus. One enemy of the leaf cutter ant is a fly that lays its eggs on the ant's back. When the eggs hatch, the larvae crawl out and eat the leaf cutter ant's brains. Smaller worker ants called "minima" ride on the backs of the larger ants and use their pincers to protect the larger ants from the flies.

Army ants

Army ants are the most dangerous of all ants because of their powerful jaws. They usually eat frogs, lizards, snakes, and nesting birds, but they can also devour a horse in just a few hours. An army ant's jaws are so powerful that indigenous people used to place the ant on an open wound, squeeze it from behind so that the ant would bite down, cut off the ant's back half, then leave the ant's jaws clamped on like a stitch until the wound healed.

Birds, big and small

Birds as small as the hummingbird and as large as the eagle live in the rainforest. One of the world's largest birds, the harpy eagle, weighs up to 20 pounds (9 kilograms) and has a wingspan of up to seven feet (2.1 meters). When the harpy eagle spots a parrot, monkey, or sloth, it swoops down and uses its powerful talons, which are larger than the claws of a grizzly bear, to pull its meal from the tree. The rainforest is also home to 40 kinds of toucans. Toucans have two toes facing forward and two toes facing backward that allow them to grip tree branches. Their light bills are four times larger than their heads. They use their bills to grab fruit from the trees, and then they eat the fruit whole.

Ferocious fish

Some of the world's largest freshwater fish, such as the piraiba, which is a type of catfish, and the pirarucu, live in the rivers of the Amazon basin. Pirarucu grow up to ten feet (3 meters) long and weigh up to 300 pounds (135 kilograms). They are born with gills, but the gills disappear as the fish mature. Then, pirarucu breathe through an organ similar to lungs.

Of the eighteen kinds of piranha in the rivers of the rainforest, only four are dangerous to humans. They attack people if their normal food supply is low, but this is rare.

Piranha have powerful jaw muscles and razor-sharp teeth, which they use to eat fruit, seeds, fish, birds, and larger animals.

The jaguar is one of the largest predators in the rainforest. Its spotted fur blends in with leaves and shadows, allowing it to sneak up on its prey.

The vanishing Amazon

The Amazon rainforest is home to indigenous people whose ancestors have lived there for thousands of years. Over the past few hundred years, Brazilians of other backgrounds have also come to the rainforest to make a living tapping rubber trees, farming small plots of land, and collecting Brazil nuts. For the past 30 years, the government has encouraged Brazilian and foreign-owned companies to log, mine, and farm in the Amazon basin. These activities have destroyed large areas of the rainforest, prompting people in Brazil and around the world to demand that the government prevent further destruction.

The effects of mining

Not only do mines replace valuable areas of rainforest, but the mercury that miners use harms the environment. Miners use mercury to separate gold from mud. Mercury that enters rivers mixes with the dirt and mud at the bottom of the rivers and makes the water cloudy. Light cannot reach plants in the water, so they die. As well, fish that swallow mercury become sick, and animals and humans that eat the fish are poisoned.

The greenhouse effect

Rainforest trees absorb carbon dioxide, a colorless, odorless gas in the earth's atmosphere. With less rainforest trees to absorb the carbon dioxide, the gas stays in the atmosphere, trapping the sun's heat and raising the earth's temperature. This is called the greenhouse effect. Because of the increase in temperature, polar ice caps melt and the level of the world's oceans rises. Scientists and **environmentalists** fear that, over time, the rising oceans could flood populated coastal areas and turn other areas into deserts.

(top) Large sections of rainforest are burned to make room for crops or cattle pastures. Often, the wind causes the fires to spread through the rainforest, and they burn uncontrollably for months.

Mercury from mining pollutes the Amazon's waters and turns them a sickly reddish-brown color. Mercury is also released into the air as gas, and people who breathe in the gas become sick.

Conservation efforts

By 1988, the Amazon rainforest was disappearing at a rate of 8,300 square miles (21,500 square kilometers) a year. Several species of plants and animals disappeared every day. Environmentalists in Brazil and around the world were outraged. Rock singer Sting and his wife, Trudie Styler, are among the many people who brought attention to the disappearing Amazon. They founded Rainforest Foundation International (RFI). This organization holds events to support indigenous people who are working to protect their environment.

Pressure from organizations such as RFI has resulted in laws to control economic activity in the rainforest. Loggers are required to plant new trees where they cut. Roads and power plants must be built in ways that do not destroy the environment. People in the rainforest are being encouraged to find ways to make a living without chopping down trees and polluting the rivers. These measures are having some effect. In 2000, only 7,037 square miles (18,226 square kilometers) of rainforest disappeared.

Chico Mendes

Chico Mendes (1944–1988) was a rubber tapper from the state of Acre, in the western Amazon, who worked to protect the rainforest. When ranchers and farmers began to cut down large areas of rainforest, Mendes organized other rubber tappers into a **union**. Members of the union protested against the ranchers and farmers by standing in the way of trucks carrying equipment to clear the forest. In 1988, an angry rancher and his son murdered Chico Mendes. Mendes' murder brought international attention to the vanishing rainforests and forced Brazil's government to find ways to protect and preserve the Amazon.

Chico Mendes became famous for his courage in protecting the rainforest. In his memory, an award is given each year to a person who works to preserve the environment.

# Glossary

ancestor A person from whom one is descended

colony An area controlled by a distant country

convert To change one's religion, faith, or beliefs

currency Money

descendant A person who can trace his or her family roots to a certain family or group

environmentalist A person who tries to protect nature

ethnic Describing people from a certain country or race

extract To remove

fertile Able to produce abundant crops or vegetation

fungus A living thing that gets food from decaying material

generator A machine that produces electricity

geologist A person who studies rocks and materials in the earth's surface

gorge A deep narrow valley with steep sides

highland A mountainous part of a country

homeland A country that is identified with a particular people or ethnic group

indigenous Native to a country

intermarry To marry someone of a different religion or ethnic group

irrigate To supply water to land

livestock Farm animals

logging The process of cutting down trees

mercury A silver-colored metal which is liquid at room temperature

mesa A broad, flat plain with cliff-like sides

mineral A naturally occurring, non-living substance obtained through mining

natural resource A material found in nature, such as oil, coal, minerals, or timber

nervous system The brain and the nerves, which send messages to control movement and feeling

nuclear power Energy that is created when atoms come together or split apart

plain A large area of flat land

plantation A large farm on which crops such as cotton and sugar are grown

plateau An area of flat land that is higher than the surrounding land

predator An animal that kills and eats other animals

prospector A person who explores an area for minerals or precious metals

rainforest A tropical forest with high rainfall

reef A rocky ledge just below the surface of the sea

resistance The body's natural ability to fight off disease

saint A person through whom God performs miracles, according to the Christian Church

tributary A river or stream that flows into a larger river or lake

turbine An engine that uses water, steam, or air to make it move

union An organization that protects the rights of workers

# Index

1 2 3 4 5 6 7 8 9 0   Printed in the USA   0 9 8 7 6 5 4 3

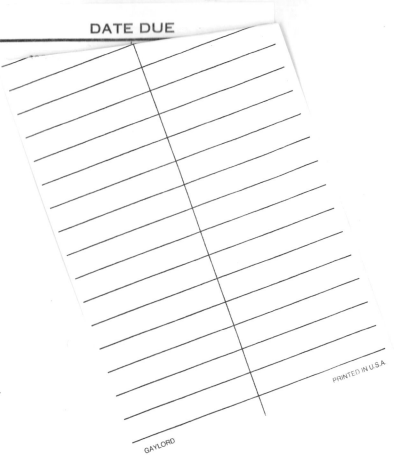

DATE DUE

PRINTED IN U.S.A.

GAYLORD